IMAGES
of Sport

BRISTOL CITY
FOOTBALL CLUB
1894-1967

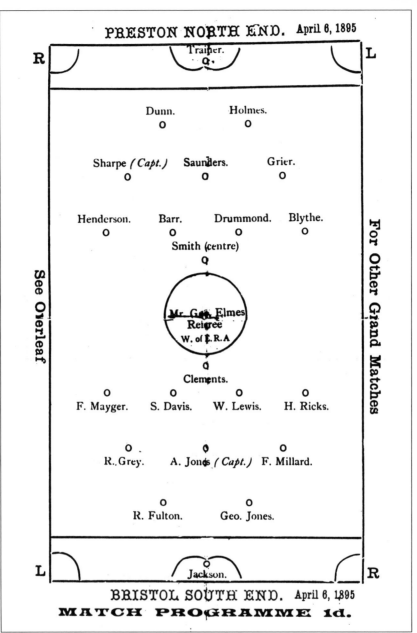

PRESTON NORTH END. April 6, 1895

R   Trainer.
               Q.   L

Dunn.   Holmes.
O   O

Sharpe *(Capt.)*   Saunders.   Grier.
O   O   O

Henderson.   Barr.   Drummond.   Blythe.
O   O   O   O

Smith (centre)
Q

Mr. Geo. Elmes
Referee
W. of E.R.A

Q

Clements.
Q

O   O   O   O
F. Mayger.   S. Davis.   W. Lewis.   H. Ricks.

O   Q   O
R. Grey.   A. Jones *(Capt.)*   F. Millard.

O   O
R. Fulton.   Geo. Jones.

L   Jackson.   R

BRISTOL SOUTH END. April 6, 1895
MATCH PROGRAMME 1d.

See Overleaf   *For Other Grand Matches*

Bristol South End programme, 1894/95. This, the earliest known South End programme, was found in a scrapbook kept by Frank Mayger who played on the left wing in this match against Preston North End. The single-sheet issue is printed on light (possibly faded) pink paper. The reverse gives the following information on forthcoming fixtures: 'Bristol South End FC Grand Holiday Attractions all at St John's Lane, Bedminster. Apr 10 – Bristol South League; Apr 12 – Hereford Thistle; Apr 13 – London Welsh; Apr 15 – 1st Scots Guards; Apr 16 – Tottenham Hotspur; Apr 20 – Cardiff; Apr 27 – Eastville Rovers. For Further Particulars see Bills.' It is not known whether programmes were issued for every match at this time. However, comments in City's handbook at the turn of the last century makes clear that programmes were issued in 1899/1900, though sometime later the practice was discontinued before being revived at the start of 1906/07.

IMAGES
of Sport

BRISTOL CITY
FOOTBALL CLUB
1894-1967

Compiled by
Tom Hopegood

TEMPUS

First published 2000
Copyright © Tom Hopegood, 2000

Tempus Publishing Limited
The Mill, Brimscombe Port,
Stroud, Gloucestershire, GL5 2QG

ISBN 0 7524 2040 2

Typesetting and origination by
Tempus Publishing Limited
Printed in Great Britain by
Midway Clark Printing, Wiltshire

*This work is dedicated to my uncle, David Frederick Hopegood, who planted
and nurtured the seed of my fascination with Bristol City Football Club.*

Also available from Tempus Publishing

Bristol Rovers FC	Mike Jay	0 7524 1150 0
Devon Derbies	Mike Holgate	0 7524 1898 X
Exeter City FC: 1904-1994	Dave Fisher/Gerald Gosling	0 7524 1167 5
Final Tie	Norman Shiel	0 7524 1669 3
The Football Programme	John Litster	0 7524 1855 6
Forever England	Mark Shaoul/Tony Williamson	0 7524 2042 9
Grecian Voices	Dave Fisher/Gerald Gosling	0 7524 1621 9
Oxford United FC	Jon Murray	0 7524 1183 7
Plymouth Argyle FC	Gordon Sparks	0 7524 1185 3
Reading FC: 1871-1997	David Downs	0 7524 1061 X
Swindon Town FC	Richard Mattick	Summer 2000
Torquay United FC	Mike Holgate	0 7524 1814 9
1966 World Cup	Norman Shiel	0 7524 2045 3
Bristol RFC	Mark Hoskins/Dave Fox	0 7524 1875 0
Cardiff RFC	Duncan Gardiner/Alan Evans	0 7524 1608 1
The Five Nations Story	David Hands	0 7524 1851 3

Contents

BRISTOL CITY AUTOGRAPHS

City players' autographs, 1953/54. These were taken from the programme for the Arsenal floodlight match which City won 3-1 on 30 March 1954 in front of a 28,991 crowd.

Foreword

Whilst there have been a number of narrative histories on Bristol City FC in recent years, what has been missing is a pictorial record. Fortunately, this void has now been rectified by the publication of this book, which I have the pleasure of introducing.

This work, which includes the glories of the First Division days in the Edwardian era, as well as the period when the legendary John Atyeo was at Ashton Gate, has reawakened memories of my time at the club.

I was fortunate enough to play regularly with big John and, following relegation to the Third Division in 1960, was part of an inside forward trio that is fondly remembered by many City fans. Goals were certainly in plentiful supply at this time, with 50 or more home League goals being scored for five successive seasons, whilst a 4-2 win over Reading at the end of 1962/63 brought up the century mark for the campaign.

Those were happy days that included some stirring FA Cup performances. A 1-0 win at Plymouth, an 11-0 demolition of Chichester City, an exciting 5-2 success at Hereford and two thrilling tussles with Aston Villa were some of the highlights before I departed City's promotion-bound side to join Rotherham United in early 1965. I wasn't away for long though as my new club were the visitors for the opening match of the following season, when City gained a rather fortunate 2-1 victory.

Bobby 'Shadow' Williams

6

Introduction

Whilst the name of Bristol City Football Club has been known throughout the football world since 1897, the origins of the club go back further than that. Founded as Bristol South End on 12 April 1894, they changed their name on adopting professionalism and gaining admission to the First Division of the Southern League.

Narrowly missing out on the Championship in 1897/98 and 1898/99, amalgamation with local rivals Bedminster, who had been founded as Southville in 1887, followed at the conclusion of a poor campaign in 1899/1900. The reinvigorated club almost secured Southern League honours in 1900/01, despite sharing their home games between City's St John's Lane ground and Bedminster's Ashton Gate.

City's disappointment at missing out to Southampton for the top spot was possibly lessened by being successful in gaining election to the Second Division of the Football League. This brought to an end the experiment of using both grounds, but it wasn't until the start of the 1904/05 season that St John's Lane was eventually vacated for a revamped Ashton Gate.

Finishing sixth in their initial League campaign in 1901/02, three successive fourth placings then followed before promotion was achieved when the Second Division Championship was won with new records in respect of games won (30) and points gained (66). City's fourteen successive League wins in this 1905/06 season was also a record, equalling Manchester United's achievement of the previous year, a feat that has only subsequently been matched by Preston North End in 1950/51.

The record breaking continued in the top flight as City became the first newly promoted club to narrowly miss out on the Championship; this wasn't equalled until 1936/37 when Charlton Athletic also finished as runners-up in their initial First Division season, though in 1961/62 Ipswich Town rewrote the record books by clinching top spot honours at their first attempt.

When they reached the FA Cup final in 1909, many thought City as being fully established in the top flight, despite losing 0-1 to Manchester United at Crystal Palace in front of a 71,401 crowd (destined to remain the largest gathering ever to witness a Bristol City match for almost ninety-one years). Unfortunately, two years later a 0-1 home defeat by Everton in the final game of the season brought relegation to the Second Division.

At this time the Football League was comprised of only two divisions and City had their work cut out in avoiding having to seek re-election in 1911/12 and 1912/13. With the extension of the League after the First World War, City found themselves in the Third Division (South) in 1922/23. In between times though they had a measure of success, reaching the semi-final of the FA Cup in 1920 – when their injury-hit side were somewhat unfortunate in losing 1-2 against

Huddersfield Town at Stamford Bridge – and almost gaining promotion the following season before having to settle for third place behind the champions Birmingham and runners-up Cardiff City.

Their stay in the Third Division was brief as the divisional championship was immediately won, but tenure back in higher company was equally brief as a final total of just 29 points brought demotion yet again. This time it took three attempts before Second Division status was regained in 1926/27 when a new record of 62 points for the Third Division (South) secured City the Championship.

Five seasons, of which the last four were of perpetual struggle, was the extent of City's sojourn this time, before relegation was the inevitable outcome of finishing the 1931/32 campaign with a paltry total of 23 points. Even worse was to come though as, apart from finishing as runners-up in 1937/38, financially threatened City struggled right up to the start of the Second World War in 1939. The only successes in this period were in winning the Welsh Cup in 1934 (beating Tranmere Rovers in a replay 3-0), an FA Cup run the following season that brought the First Division scalp of Portsmouth and reaching the final of the Third Division (South) Cup in 1938.

After the war, City started well and finished third in 1946/47, when their goal-hungry attack, with 94 goals, were the top scorers in the Third Division (South). Despite this form it wasn't until 1954/55 that promotion was achieved, when their total of 70 points equalled the record set by Nottingham Forest four seasons earlier. In the Second Division the following year, City looked almost certainties for promotion when top of the table at Christmas, but form then dipped and they eventually had to settle for eleventh place. After this they struggled again until the appointment of the legendary Peter Doherty as manager in January 1958.

One of the greatest players of his generation, Doherty had cut his managerial teeth by taking Doncaster Rovers into the Second Division, as well as being boss of the Northern Ireland side. Saving City from the drop in 1957/58 and then guiding Northern Ireland into the quarter-finals of the World Cup in Sweden during the close season, he worked the oracle for 1958/59. He had City playing great football and looking worthy promotion candidates early on, but again poor form after the turn of the year cost the club dear.

Changes had to be made, but unfortunately many of City's long-serving local players objected. Their side, strengthened by record signings from Barnsley of Malcolm Graham and John McCann, as well as the acquisition of Doncaster's Tommy Cavanagh and Northern Ireland international Tommy Casey from Portsmouth, which was touted as one of the promotion favourites, but sank without trace as they became riven by internal dissension in what became known as the 'split camp affair'. Doherty became the victim of player power and was dismissed in early March 1960, but even though results improved somewhat after this it was not enough to save them.

Under new manager Fred Ford in what was, following changes that had been made at the end of the 1957/58 campaign, now a national Third Division, City struggled throughout 1960/61 before eventually finishing in fourteen place. The season's highlight was beating Chichester City 11-0 in the FA Cup – City's highest ever score in the competition. Ford built an attack-minded sided and the four seasons that followed in the Third Division brought some exciting times. Even the disappointing 1962/63 campaign had its highlights as, despite finishing a lowly fourteenth, City managed to notch a century of goals. Twice finishing fifth, City eventually achieved promotion in 1964/65 when, having only suffered one defeat in a run of fifteen games to the end of the season, they finished as runners-up, pipping Mansfield Town by virtue of a better goal average.

Back in the Second Division, City were promotion challengers throughout the 1965/66 campaign, their final placing of fifth being their highest in this division for forty-five years. Unfortunately, the following season brought back the familiar struggle, though the signings of John Quigley, Chris Crowe and Hugh McIlmoyle had the public expecting great things for 1967/68.

One

Amateur Days

Bristol South End AFC, 1894/95. South End, wearing red shirts and navy blue shorts, photographed prior to their first ever game, which was against Swindon Town in front of a 3,500 crowd at St John's Lane on 1 September 1894. They lost the fixture 2-4. From left to right (players only), back row: A. Taylor, A.E.Y. Trestrail, J.W. Welham. Middle row: F. Sankey Davis, Arthur Jones (captain), George Jones. Front row: R. Walters, G. Fry, W. Lewis, Hamlet Horatio ('Hammer') Clements, Frank E. Mayger. This picture was taken from the *Bristol Sports Post* of 3 September 1932.

Football advertisements in the *Bristol Times & Mirror* of 12 October 1894. On the Saturday, Bristol South End beat Wells 4-0 in front of a 1,300 crowd, whilst Aston Villa notched up an easy success the following Monday when the new St George ground was opened.

This is the programme for the first match on the new St George ground, which Villa won 8-0 on 15 October 1894. However, the Bristol & District League XI didn't have to wait very long for revenge. In front of 5,380 spectators, who paid a total of £143 1s 6d, at the same venue on 7 April 1896 they pulled off a famous 2-0 victory (though by then they had changed their name to the Western League).

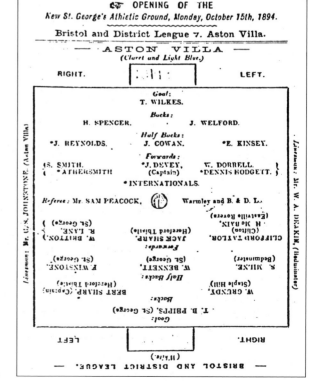

St John's Lane, 1894/95. The action, photographed from Windmill Hill (then known as Mutton Hill), is probably from the prestigious friendly against Preston North End on 6 April which the famous visitors won 6-1 in front of 3,500 spectators. This view – from what was dubbed 'scroungers' gallery' – was eventually blocked out when the club hoisted canvas sheets on a series of 30ft poles, such sheets also being used as advertising hoardings. (This photograph belongs to Ron Cranfield of Portishead.)

FOOTBALL.

THIS DAY.

AMATEUR CUP COMPETITION

PROPER (FIRST ROUND).

January 30th, at 2.30,

At ST. JOHN'S LANE, BEDMINSTER.

First Visit to Bristol of

THE OLD CARTHUSIANS

(The finest Amateur Team in the Country) v.

BRISTOL SOUTH END.

Admission 6d.; Boys, 3d.; Enclosure 3d. extra. Everybody Pay.

BRISTOL SOUTH PRIZE BAND will attend.

☞ The Old Carthusian Team will consist entirely of Internationals and University Men.

Referee—P. R. McLaughlin, Esq., Southampton. 127

Bristol South End v. Old Carthusians, 1896/97. South End lost this Amateur Cup clash 0-10 in front of a 1,700 crowd at St John's Lane on 30 January 1897.

Bedminster AFC, 1892/93. This is the Bedminster team, in their colours of maroon and old gold, that drew 0-0 with St George in a friendly at Greenway Bush Lane in front of 800 spectators on 3 April 1893. From left to right (players only), middle row: A. King, G.E. Jones, Charlie E. Gyles, James W. Wallace, F.E. Skeates, Fred W. Gyles, W.G. Griffiths. Front row: Arthur Jones, S.J. ('Scottie') Milne, Revd A.B. Macfarlane (captain), Frank Mayger. This photograph is from Frank Mayger's scrapbook.

Derby County v. West Bromwich Albion at Ashton Gate, 1896/97. Goals from J. Goodall and Bloomer brought Derby a 2-1 win for a purse of not less than ten guineas in front of a 5,000 crowd, paying receipts of £123 13s 6d.

Two
Professionalism

Southern League runners-up, 1897/98. This Bristol City side, in red shirts and white shorts, beat
Wolverton LNWR 7-4 in front of 4,000 spectators at St John's Lane on their Southern League debut
on 11 September 1897. From left to right, back row: Harry Davy, Sam Hollis (manager), Hugh
Monteith. Middle row: George Mann, Billy ('Sandy') Higgins (captain), Finlay Sinclair, A. John
('Jack') Hamilton. Front: Tom Wyllie, Albert Carnelly, Alex Caie, Patrick ('Paddy') O'Brien, John
('Jock') Russell. This photograph was a free insert with *The Bristol Magpie* of 30 September 1897.

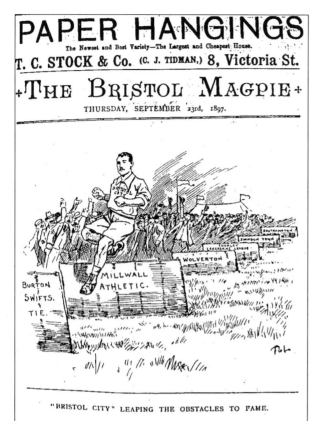

PAPER HANGINGS
The Newest and Best Variety—The Largest and Cheapest House.

T. C. STOCK & Co. (C. J. TIDMAN,) 8, Victoria St.

+THE BRISTOL MAGPIE+

THURSDAY, SEPTEMBER 23rd, 1897.

"BRISTOL CITY" LEAPING THE OBSTACLES TO FAME.

The earliest known local football cartoon from the 1897/98 season. City's winning start to their professional career was celebrated by *The Bristol Magpie* with this cartoon on the front cover of their issue of 23 September 1897.

Bristol City *v.* Southampton, 1897/98. The Saint's retreat from St John's Lane after suffering a 2-5 defeat on 15 January 1898 – in front of a new record Southern League crowd of 12,170 who generated receipts of £379 16s 2d – is likened to Napoleon's retreat from Moscow in this brilliant cartoon which appeared in *The Bristol Magpie* five days later.

THE RETREAT FROM MOSCOW, OR THE DEFEAT OF THE SOUTHAMPTON CHAMPIONS.

Bedminster, 1898/99. This photograph of Bedminster's first professional side appeared in *The Bristol Magpie* on two occasions during this season – 22 September 1898 and 16 March 1899. Left to right, back row: S. Mountford (trainer), Bob Kelso (captain), W. Cox, James Whitehouse, G. Brooks, Robert Crone. Middle row: James Lamont, D. Proudfoot, B. Livesey, Alex Stewart, W. McDonald. Front row: Malcolm McVean, J. Bell, W. Massie, J. Leonard, David Copeland, R. Gray.

Bristol City Football Annual, 1897/98. This was Bristol City's first season as a professional club, following the changing of their name from Bristol South End.

Southern League runners-up, 1898/99. This picture shows City with the Gloucestershire Cup, which they won for the first time the previous season when Warmley were defeated 2-1 at Eastville in front of 11,186 spectators on 11 April. Left to right, back row: Dick Batten (trainer), Phil Britton, Harry Davy, Hugh Monteith, Sam Hollis (manager), Alex Caie, Billy Stewart (captain), George Mann. Middle row: Arthur Potter, George Barker, Billy Jones, John McLean, Jack Hamilton, John Murphy. Front row: Billy Langham, Albert Carnelly, Pat Finnerhan, James Stevenson, 'Paddy' O'Brien, 'Jock' Russell.

The Bristol City handbook, 1899/1900. This was a more substantial publication than that issued two years previously, despite being reduced in price by 1d.

St John's Lane ground, 1898/99. This sketch appeared in *The Bristol Magpie* of 20 April 1899. Note the canvas screens at the end of the ground.

The Bristol Magpie of 4 May 1899. City lost the Championship by allowing the Saints to recover from a 0-2 half-time deficit to clinch a 4-3 win on 29 Apr 1899 in front of a new record 13,000 crowd, who paid a total of £440, at St John's Lane.

Bristol City, 1898/99. This photograph is a bit of a mystery with City in unfamiliar halved shirts and with many players it has not been possible to identify. The picture, which was taken at the rear of the St John's Lane Grandstand, is unusual in that the players appear to be arranged in their match positions. From left to right, back row: unknown (goalkeeper). Third row: unknown (right-back), George Barker? (left-back). Second row: Alex Caie (right half), Unknown (centre half), Jack Hamilton (left half). Front row: unknown (right wing), Albert Carnelly (inside right), unknown (centre forward), 'Paddy' O'Brien (inside left), 'Jock' Russell (left wing). (This photograph belongs to David Wring of Failand.)

Millwall v. Bristol City programme, 1899/1900. City lost this Southern District Combination game 0-1 in front of a 5,000 crowd on 16 April 1900.

Bedminster, 1899/1900. Left to right, back row: Mountford (trainer), Robert Crone, George Toone, Robert H. Davies, Sam Hollis (manager). Middle row: Charles Bramley, W.H. Davies, W. Draycott, Hugh Wilson, Peter Chambers, Ayre. Front: W.H. Burland (financial secretary), Michael Whelan, Albert Flewitt, Tommy Boucher, Francis Becton, Alfred Geddes, A. Saxton.

'That Ten Pound Note', 1900/01. Seeking a prize at Ashton Gate as recorded by *The Bristol Magpie* of 25 October 1900. It was for this season only that City's matches were shared between Ashton Gate and St John's Lane.

The Bristol Magpie

THURSDAY, DECEMBER 27th, 1900.

FATHER CHRISTMAS : "Here's a couple of good hard nuts to crack !"

'Father Christmas', as drawn by *The Bristol Magpie* of 27 December 1900. Unfortunately, City were destined to lose their first round FA Cup match against Reading 1-2 at the County Ground, Swindon, in a second replay after drawing 1-1 away and 0-0 at home.

Portsmouth *v.* Bristol City, 1900/01. The programme for this Western League game, which City lost 0-3 in front of 2,000 spectators, is incorrectly dated 1900.

Three
Into the League

Bristol City, 1901/02. Left to right, back row: Billy Jones, James Robertson, Wally Moles, Billy Tuft, Peter Chambers, Robert Davies. Middle row: Robert Crone (trainer), Joseph Bradbury, Joseph Connor, Tommy Boucher, 'Paddy' O'Brien, Arthur Flynn, Sam Hollis (manager). Front row: Walter Cookson, John McLean, Steve Jones. This image comes from *The Golden Penny Football Album* for the 1901/02 season.

'Ashton Gate or St John's Lane?', a cartoon from *The Bristol Magpie* of 26 September 1901 as Bristol City ponder over which ground to use. They resolved to keep St John's Lane as their headquarters, a decision in line with the wishes of the majority of their supporters as well as a poll in *The Bristol Magpie* which produced a vote 582 to 470 in favour of St John's Lane, though three years later it was eventually decided to move to Ashton Gate.

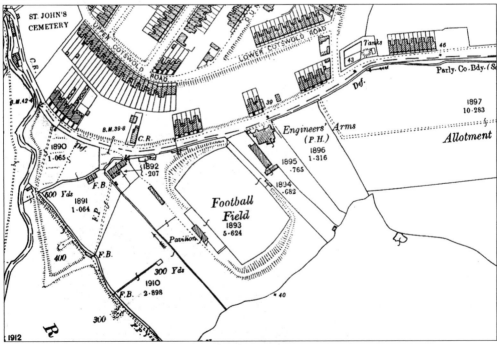

This plan of City's St John's Lane ground is from 1902.

Bristol City *v.* Woolwich Arsenal, 1901/02. This action comes from City's first season in the Football League. In front of a 10,500 St John's Lane crowd on 26 October 1901, City (in white) surrendered their unbeaten home record as Woolwich Arsenal recorded a 3-0 win. Note the canvas screens in the background blocking off the view from Mutton Hill. This image comes from the *Black & White Budget* of 9 November 1901.

Tottenham Hotspur *v.* Bristol City, 1902/03. Alas, City were unable to emulate Bristol RFC's great victory over Gloucester, as they lost 0-1 at Tottenham in the FA Cup on 21 February 1903.

Bristol City, 1902/03. Left to right, back row: Billy Tuft, Harry Clay, Peter Chambers, George Lewis, Robert Davies. Middle row: Sam Hollis (manager), Billy Jones (captain), Michael Good, Alf Dean, Tommy Boucher, Herbert Banks, Robert Crone (trainer). Front row: Dick Wombwell, Walter Leigh, Charles Barnes. This photograph comes from *Maquire's Photo Album of Famous Football Teams*.

Bristol City and Bristol Rovers, 1902/03. Despite the good start illustrated by this cartoon, neither City or Rovers won League honours during this campaign. This cartoon was published in *The Bristol Magpie* of 2 October 1902.

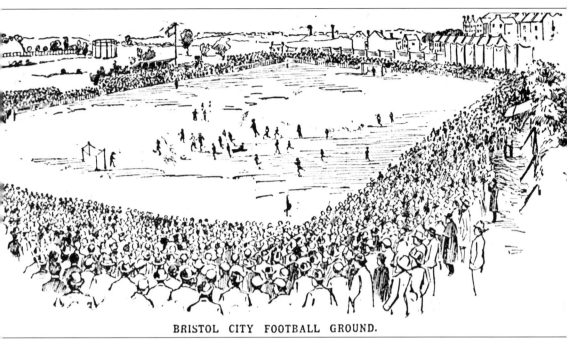

BRISTOL CITY FOOTBALL GROUND.

St John's Lane, 1902/03. This sketch of City's 1-0 win over Woolwich Arsenal in front of 12,024 spectators on 4 October 1902 appeared in the *Bristol Observer* four weeks after the match.

Bristol City v. Leicester Fosse, 1902/03. City won 6-1 in front of a 5,000 crowd on 7 March 1903.

FINAL EDITION.

'EVENING NEWS' OFFICE, 6 P.M.

ENGLISH LEAGUE MATCH

AT ST. JOHN'S LANE.

TO-MORROW AT 3.30,

LEICESTER FOSSE

v.

BRISTOL CITY

Admission 6d.   Stands and Enclosures Extra

SPANNING THE USK

NEWPORT'S
REMARKABLE
SCHEME.

SEE

THE BRISTOL OBSERVER

NOW READY.

SECOND EDITION TO-MORROW.

Bristol City, 1903/04. Left to right, back row: Alf Gilson, Billy Tuft, Harry Clay, Phil Bach. Middle row: Sam Hollis (manager), Charles Barnes, Billy Jones, Jim Hosie, Peter Chambers, Dick Batten (trainer). Front row: Alf Dean, Albert Fisher, Fred Corbett, Jack Morris, Dick Wombwell.

FINAL FOOTBALL MATCH

ON THE

ST. JOHN'S LANE GROUND.

TO-MORROW, AT 3.30.

BRISTOL CITY

(Winners Gloucester County Cup)

V

BRISTOL CITY RES.

(Winners Bristol Charity Bowl and Western League Cup).

ADMISSION 6d. Stand and Enclosures Extra.

City bid farewell to St John's Lane by beating their reserves 3-2 in this game played on 30 April 1904. The last League match on the ground had been played a week previously when Burslem Port Vale were beaten 2-1 in front of 4,000 spectators.

Bristol City, 1904/05. Left to right, back row: William Panes Kingston (chairman), Harry Thickett, Billy Tuft, Harry Clay, Andrew Hargett, Billy Demmery, Sam Hollis (manager). Middle row: D. Thomas (director), Alf Gilson, Billy Jones, Jim Hosie, Albert Fisher, Peter Chambers, Freddie Fenton, Frank Noot Bacon (director), Dick Batten (trainer). Front row: Alf Dean, Fred Corbett, Sammy Gilligan, Alf Capes, Dick Wombwell. This team group photograph was taken from *The Daily Graphic Football Album*.

Match advertising from 1904/05. City, playing in green shirts, beat Woolwich Arsenal 1-0 in their FA Cup replay watched by 11,176 fans, paying receipts of £298 19s 3d, on 8 February 1905.

FINAL EDITION.

FOOTBALL NOTICES.

FOOTBALL AT STAPLETON ROAD.

REPLAY ENGLISH CUP TIE.

BOLTON WANDERERS

v

BRISTOL ROVERS.

WEDNESDAY, FEBRUARY 8TH.
KICK-OFF 3 P.M.

EVERYBODY PAY TO ALL PARTS OF GROUND. PRICES AS USUAL. NO EXTRA CHARGES.

BRISTOL CITY FOOTBALL GROUND, ASHTON GATE.

ENGLISH CUP.
FIRST ROUND.   REPLAY TIE.

WOOLWICH ARSENAL

v.

BRISTOL CITY.

WEDNESDAY NEXT, FEB. 8TH, AT 3.15.

ADMISSION: To Ground, 6d; No. 2 Covered Stand and Enclosure, 6d extra; Grand Stand and Enclosure, 1s extra.

EVERYBODY PAY (except Life Members).

Bristol City, Second Division Champions, 1905/06. Left to right, back row: Harry Thickett (manager), Billy Jones, Billy Tuft, Archie Annan, Arthur Spear, Harry Clay, Joe Cottle, W. Boulton, Pat Hanlin, Dick Batten (trainer). Front row: Sammy Gilligan, Walter 'Cocky' Bennett, Billy Maxwell, Peter Chambers, Andy Burton, Pat Hilton, Billy Ingham, Charles Stevens. On the ground: Billy Wedlock, Freddie Fenton.

Bristol City v. Leicester Fosse, 1905/06. The Fossils proved to be anything but sacrificial victims as they shocked City at Ashton Gate by winning 2-1 in front of 8,000 fans on 17 February 1906. This was published in *The Bristol Magpie* on 15 February 1906.

'Bristol City Well On The Way', 1906/07. City's all-conquering 1905/06 side went on to do great things the following season, when the League Championship was within their grasp, as depicted by *The Bristol Magpie* of 18 April 1907.

Bristol City, perhaps all dressed up for a night on the town, 1905/06. Left to right, back row: Billy Maxwell, Arthur Spear, 'Cocky' Bennett, Dick Batten (trainer). Middle row: Frank Noot Bacon (director), Archie Annan, Harry Clay, Joe Cottle, Pat Hanlin, Harry Thickett (manager). Front row: Frank Hilton, Freddie Fenton, Billy Wedlock (captain), Andy Burton, Sammy Gilligan. This picture appeared in *Association Football & The Men Who Made It*.

Promotion banquet, 1905/06. City celebrated their promotion to the top flight with a sumptuous dinner at the Royal Hotel, College Green.

The toast list and programme of events from the celebratory meal.

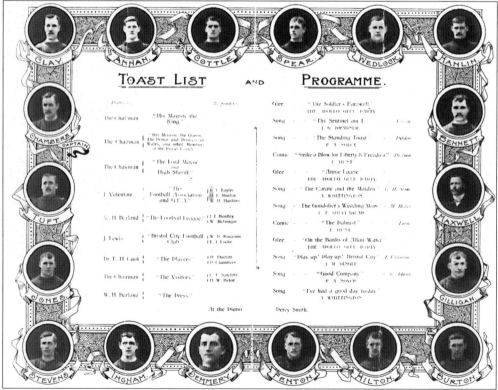

Four
With the Elite

Bristol City at the start of the 1906/07 season, showing off the Gloucestershire Cup and the Second Division Shield. Left to right, back row: E.J. Locke (honorary secretary), Frank Noot Bacon (director), William Panes Kingston (chairman), Billie Burland (vice-chairman), Joseph Daveridge (director). Middle row: Harry Thickett (manager), Billy Tuft, Gale, Archie Annan, Harry Clay, Billy Demmery, Joe Cottle, Rueben Marr, F.V. Larway (director), Dick Batten (trainer). Front row: 'Cocky' Bennett, Billy Maxwell, Sammy Gilligan, Peter Chambers, Andy Burton, Pat Hilton, Billy Wedlock (captain). On the ground: Arthur Spear, Billy Ingham, Fred Staniforth, Fred Connelly.

Bristol City *v.* Manchester United, 1906/07. City's first ever match in the top flight brought defeat at the hands of Manchester United, who gained revenge for missing out on the Second Division Championship with a 2-1 success at Ashton Gate in front of 21,000 crowd on 1 September 1906. (This postcard belongs to Manchester United supporter James Thomas.)

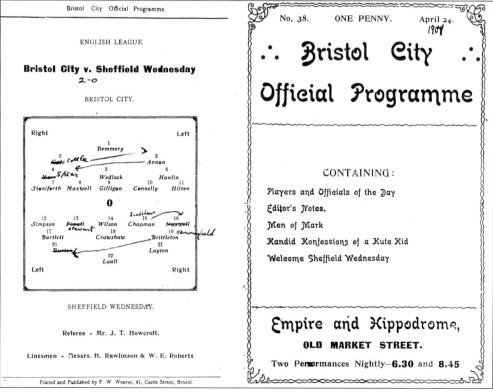

Bristol City *v.* Sheffield Wednesday programme, 1906/07. City beat Wednesday 2-0 in front of a 16,000 crowd on 24 April 1907 to go second in the First Division table.

Stoke v. Bristol City, 1906/07. This line-up brought City their first ever win in the top flight, beating Stoke 3-0 in front of an 8,000 away crowd on 8 September 1906. Left to right, back row: Dick Batten (trainer), Fred Staniforth, Rueben Marr, Archie Annan, Joe Cottle, Frank Noot Bacon (director), F.V. Larway (director), Harry Thickett (manager). Front row: 'Cocky' Bennett, Billy Maxwell, Sammy Gilligan, Harry Clay, Andy Burton, Frank Hilton, Billy Wedlock (captain), Pat Hanlin.

City star Billy Wedlock. An inspiring captain for City, he scored twice in 26 appearances for England between 1906 and 1914. A centre half, Wedlock played on at Ashton Gate until the end of the 1920/21 season.

Bristol City, 1907/08. Left to right, back row: Dick Batten (trainer), Tom Gale, Willis Rippon, Bob Young, Billy Demmery, Arthur Spear, Frank Noot Bacon (director), Harry Thickett (manager). Middle row: Rueben Marr, Fred Staniforth, Billy Maxwell, Sammy Gilligan, Fred Connelly, Pat Hanlin, Joe Cottle, Joseph Daveridge (director). Front row: Billy Wedlock (captain), Pat Hilton.

Bristol City v. Everton, 1907/08. City won the season's opener against Everton 3-2 in front of a 14,000 Ashton Gate crowd on 2 September 1907.

Bristol City *v.* Bolton Wanderers programme, 1907/08. This Division One game was won 2-0 in front of 14,000 spectators on 18 April 1908.

Bristol City, FA Cup finalists, 1908/09. Left to right, back row: Harry Thickett (manager), F.W. Bacon (director), Archie Annan*, Bob Young, Harry Clay*, Joe Cottle*, Willis Rippon, Dick Batten (trainer). Front row: Arthur Spear*, Fred Staniforth*, Sammy Gilligan*, Billy Maxwell, Andy Burton*, Frank Hilton*, Billy Wedlock* (captain), Pat Hanlin*. Insets: Bob Hardy*, Rueben Marr. (* Denotes those that actually played in the final when injuries robbed City of the services of Rippon and Marr, who were replaced by Hilton and Hanlin).

Bristol City *v.* Norwich City, 1908/09. This, the first local football picture to appear in the Bristol newspapers, was published in the *Bristol Times & Mirror* of 27 February 1909. It shows action from the third round of the FA Cup on 20 February 1909 when City beat Southern League Norwich 2-0 in front of a 24,009 Ashton Gate crowd.

Bristol City *v.* Derby County, 1908/09. This action shot was taken during the FA Cup semi-final at Stamford Bridge on 27 March 1909. It shows Harry Clay about to clear for City while Billy Wedlock is on the extreme right.

Willis Rippon's dramatic last second equaliser from the penalty spot against Second Division Derby County. This photograph comes from the *Bristol Times & Mirror* of 29 March 1909.

The CHELSEA F.C.Chronicle

OFFICIAL PROGRAMME

of

The Chelsea Football & Athletic Company, Limited.
(Edited by "McW." of "The Wisdom Shop.")

[ENTERED AT STATIONERS' HALL.]   MEMBERS OF

The Football League (Division **1**), South Eastern League (Division 1).

VOL. IV. No. 34.   Saturday, March 27th, 1909.   [ONE PENNY.
                                                             POST FREE 1½D.

"THE HOPE OF THE SOUTH."

The Bristol Babe : "Boo-oo, I want to go to the Crystal Palace!"
The Pensioner : "Well, play with your friend first, then perhaps you shall go."

Bristol City *v.* Derby County, FA Cup semi-final programme. A crowd of 33,878, paying receipts of £2,056, saw City obtain a rather fortunate 1-1 draw.

THE GREAT CONTEST AT THE CRYSTAL PALACE.

1909

B.C.F.C.

WEDLOCK
(Captain).

MR W. P.
KINGSTON
(Chairman).

MR E. J. LOCKE
(Secretary).

STANIFORTH
(Outside Right).

COTTLE
(Left-Back).

The portraits of Mr Locke, Wedlock, Cottle, and Staniforth are from photos by Mr A. H. Wright, East Street, Bedminster.

Manchester United *v.* Bristol City, 1908/09. The great contest at The Crystal Palace as previewed by the *Bristol Observer* of 24 April 1909.

In front of a 71,401 crowd, paying receipts of £6,434 at The Crystal Palace on 24 April 1909, City, in blue shirts, kick-off the FA Cup final against Manchester United, who are turned out in white shirts with a large red 'V'.

Sandy Turnbull's shot beats Harry Clay after twenty-two minutes to secure Manchester United's first FA Cup triumph.

City 'keeper Clay under pressure again in the FA Cup final.

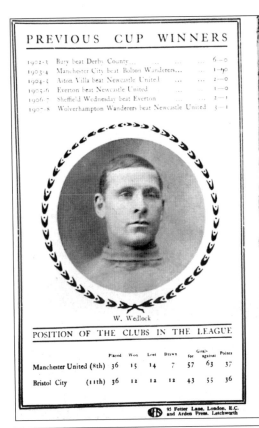

PREVIOUS CUP WINNERS

1902-3	Bury beat Derby County	6—0
1903-4	Manchester City beat Bolton Wanderers	1—0
1904-5	Aston Villa beat Newcastle United	2—0
1905-6	Everton beat Newcastle United	1—0
1906-7	Sheffield Wednesday beat Everton	2—1
1907-8	Wolverhampton Wanderers beat Newcastle United	3—1

W. Wedlock

POSITION OF THE CLUBS IN THE LEAGUE

	Played	Won	Lost	Drawn	Goals for	Goals against	Points
Manchester United (8th)	36	15	14	7	57	63	37
Bristol City (11th)	36	12	12	12	43	55	36

95 Fetter Lane, London, E.C.
and Arden Press, Letchworth

W. H. Smith & Son's
SOUVENIR CARD
OF THE
ENGLISH CUP FINAL
1909

W. Meredith

MANCHESTER UNITED v. BRISTOL CITY
PLAYED AT THE
CRYSTAL PALACE
Saturday, April 24th

PRICE: ONE PENNY

"TIT BITS" Insures you for £1,000 against Railway :: Accidents ::

PROGRAMME
— OF THE —
ENGLISH CUP FINAL, 1909.

"STORIES FOR ALL" The New All Story Weekly Every Monday, 1d.

FB Right

MANCHESTER UNITED (1)
(Colours—White Shirts and Black Knickers)

Left

MOGER

STACEY   HAYES

DUCKWORTH   ROBERTS   BELL

MEREDITH   HALSE   J. TURNBULL   A. TURNBULL   WALL

Referee   O   J. MASON, Burslem

HILTON   BURTON   GILLIGAN   HARDY   STANIFORTH

SPEAR   WEDLOCK   HANLIN

COTTLE   ANNAN

CLAY

Left

BRISTOL CITY (O)
(Colours—Blue Shirts and White Knickers)

Right

LINESMEN—J. R. Schumacher, London, and A. Green, West Bromwich

KICK-OFF 3.30 P.M.

HOW THEY GOT HERE

"THE STRAND" The Premier Illustrated Magazine :: 8d. Monthly ::	MANCHESTER UNITED		BRISTOL CITY		"THE GRAND" The All Fiction Monthly. Every Month 4½d. net.
	Brighton and Hove	1-0 Halse	Southampton	1-1 Rippon	
	Everton	1-0 Halse	Southampton	2-0 Rippon, Hardy	
	Blackburn Rovers	6-1 A.Turnbull 3	Bury	2-0 Gilligan,Burton	
		J. Turnbull 2	Bury	2-0 Gilligan	
	Burnley	0-1 Abandoned	Norwich City	2-0 Burton,Rippon	
		(15 minutes from time)	Glossop	0-0	
	Burnley (Replay)	3-2 Halse 1	Glossop	1-0 Gilligan	
		J. Turnbull 1	Derby County	0-0 Rippon	
	Newcastle United	1-0 Halse	Derby County	2-1 Rippon, Hardy	

A souvenir card (front and back) of the 1909 FA Cup final produced by W.H. Smith.

The inside of the souvenir card.

40

The official programme for the 1909 FA Cup final.

THE DIFFERENCE.
The Arsenal: What a pretty game it is to watch.
The Trio: Yes, but it's a rotten one to play at—and the last day of the season too.

'Relegation Blind Man's Buff'. Fortunately, City's 4-0 win over Nottingham Forest in front of an 11,000 Ashton Gate crowd kept them in the top flight. This comes from the *Bristol Sports Times* of 30 April 1910.

Bristol City, 1909/10. Left to right, back row: Arthur Spear, Rueben Marr, Archie Annan, Harry Clay, Joe Cottle, Pat Hanlin, Frank Hilton. Front row: Fred Staniforth, Sammy Gilligan, John Cowell, Billy Wedlock (captain), Allan Foster, Ben Shearman.

Bristol City, 1910/11. This City squad couldn't avoid relegation at the end of the season. Left to right, back row: Bob Young, Albert Osborne, Bert Chapman, Stephen Fagan, Harry Clay, John Clegg, William Bailiff, Rueben Marr, Joe Cottle, Arthur Spear. Middle row: Tom Radford, Ernie 'Ginger' Owers, Levi Copestake, Fred Staniforth, Bob Hardy, Billy Wedlock (captain), John Cowell, Andy Burton, Ben Shearman, Tom Batey, Pat Hanlin. Front row: Charlie Gould, Harry Gildea, W. Padfield, S. Mason, Allan Foster, Perry.

Five
The Aftermath

Bristol City Wednesday, 1911/12. Formed as a nursery for Bristol City in 1908, this Wednesday League side carried all before them in the competition. They notched up four consecutive cup and league doubles until their disbandment at the end of this season. Most of their home fixtures were brought off at St John's Lane, but important games were played at Ashton Gate.

The CHELSEA F.C. Chronicle

OFFICIAL PROGRAMME

of

The Chelsea Football & Athletic Company, Limited

[ENTERED AT STATIONERS' HALL]   MEMBERS OF

The Football League (Division 2).   South Eastern League (Division 1.)

VOL. VII. No. 10.   Saturday, November 4th, 1911.   ONE PENNY.
POST FREE 1½d.

CHELSEA IN CLOVER.

The Pensioner: "That little lot will show 'em there's life in the old dog yet."

Chelsea *v.* Bristol City programme, 1911/12. Billy Wedlock scored one of his rare goals as City drew this Division Two game 2-2 in front of a 25,000 crowd at Stamford Bridge on 4 November 1911.

Bristol City *v.* Bradford Park Avenue, 1912/13. A disappointing goalless draw against Bradford Park Avenue marked the start of the season. City Reserves won their South-Eastern League meeting with Swindon 1-0. This is taken from the *Bristol Evening News* of 3 September 1912.

LATE EXTRA.

FOOTBALL NOTICES.

BRISTOL CITY FOOTBALL GROUND.

WEDNESDAY, September 4, at **5.30.**
ENGLISH LEAGUE—
v. **BRADFORD.**

ADMISSION 6d. Boys 3d. Stands, &c., Extra.

SATURDAY, September 7, at **3.30.**
SOUTH-EASTERN LEAGUE—
v. **SWINDON.**

ADMISSION 4d. Boys 2d. Stands, &c., Extra.

RESERVED SEATS, 2s each.
BOOKINGS at HARRIS'S SPORTS DEPOT.
☞   HALF-PRICES AT HALF-TIME.   ☜
☞ CYCLES FREE TO GROUND at Owners' Risk.

'Shots For Goal', 1912/13. This was a regular feature which appeared in the Saturday night sports edition of the *Bristol Evening News*, this particular copy being from the paper of 29 March 1913.

Bristol City, 1913/14. Left to right, back row: Frank Noot Bacon (director), Jack Harris, Tommy Broad, Tommy Ware, John Jones, Ted Howling, Arthur Moss, John Kearns, Edwin Jones, Dick Batten (assistant trainer), G.H. Bacon (director). Middle row: W. Pont (vice-chairman), George Hedley (manager), Shortt, Fred Harrison, Tom Fuge, Billy Wedlock (captain), Ron Tasker, Fred Chapple, John 'Jock' Nicholson, Joe Palmer (trainer), Ernest Murdock (chairman). Front row: Tom Henry, Sam Irving, Edwin Burton, Tom Batey. This was a *Daily Citizen* free insert. Tragically, Ware and Burton were both killed in action during the First World War.

Bradford PA *v.* Bristol City programme, 1913/14. City went down in a controversial 3-4 defeat at Park Avenue in front of a 15,000 crowd on 13 September 1913.

Bristol City at Craven Cottage, 1913/14. City lost this Second Division game 1-3 in front of a 10,000 crowd on 20 December 1913. This was taken from *Lotinga's Weekly* of 27 December 1913.

IN BRIGHTFUL MEMORY OF

Queen's Park R. Football Team

who were beaten in the re-play of the First Round of
the ENGLISH CUP, at Bristol, by Bristol City, on

WEDNESDAY, JAN. 14TH, 1914.

Queen's Park is a clever Team, there's not the slightest doubt,
But BRISTOL CITY fairly knocked them out ;
They were determined to win, or at least to have a try,
But now they have to wait till the sweet bye-and-bye.

Never count your Chickens till they are hatched.

Score—Bristol City.................   Queen's Park.................

Bristol City *v.* Queens Park Rangers, 1913/14. Alas, chickens were indeed counted before they were hatched as, in front of a 13,781 crowd, City went down 0-2 after extra time in the Ashton Gate replay on 14 January 1914.

Bristol City *v.* Glossop, 1914/15. Glossop's last visit to Ashton Gate saw City win 3-1 in front of a 10,000 crowd on 10 October 1914. This was taken from the *Bristol Evening News* of 9 October 1914.

FOOTBALL ADVERTISEMENTS.

BRISTOL CITY FOOTBALL GROUND

TO-MORROW (SATURDAY), October 10,

AT **3.30**

ENGLISH   LEAGUE   MATCH,

V.

GLOSSOP.

ADMISSION AT USUAL PRICES.

Reserved Seats 2s each.   Booking at Harris's
Sports Depot.

☞ HALF-PRICE AT HALF-TIME.
☞ Cycles Free to Ground at Owner's Risk.

Bristol City *v.* 3rd Officer Cadets (Bristol University), 1915/16. This game, which was held in aid of War Charities, took place at Ashton Gate on 6 May 1916, when City won 6-3. Left to right, back row: F.H. Wilson, M. Bate, George Hedley (City manager), W. Cross (City), Cadet Wright, M. Wilcox (City), H.J. Martin (City), V. Bowmer, A.T. Chapman (City), C. Keys, H. Leater, T. Shrone, Lionel Manning (City), A.C. Wyness. Middle row: S.L. Welsh, H. Pughe, Laurie Banfield (City), J.H. Wardrobe, Bob Young (City), Lt Booth (Cadets captain), Billy Wedlock (City captain), H. Howe, Dickie Reader (City), G. Stansfield, Bert Neesam (City), C.Q.M.S. Ridley (linesman). Front row: Cadet Evans (linesman), Harry Kelson (City), W.A. Gardener, R. Williams (City), J.A. Shearston, R.S. Smith. A.T. Chapman had become City's record goalscorer seven days previously when he notched eight goals in a 20-1 victory against the ASC. This photograph belongs to Mr H.J. Kelson of Ashton, Bristol, who is the son of the player front left.

Bristol Rovers *v.* Bristol City, 1916/17. This cartoon from the *Bristol Sports Times* of 16 September 1916 shows that City had got their season off to a poor start the previous Saturday by losing against the Rovers 0-2 at Eastville in front of 1,200 spectators.

Bristol City, FA Cup semi-finalists, 1919/20. This side lost 1-2 against Huddersfield Town in the semi-final at Stamford Bridge on 27 March 1920. From left to right, back row: Charles Treasure, Jack Wren, Frank Vallis, Laurie Banfield, Jack Harris, 'Jock' Nicholson. Front row: Dickie Reader, Bert Neesam, Billy Wedlock (captain), Tommy Howarth, Billy Pocock.

Sergeant-Major Joe Palmer, trainer under George Hedley in 1913/14 and manager from 1919 to 1921, was photographed at Aldershot in 1913. He was also secretary/manager of Bristol Rovers for three years from May 1926.

Bristol City *v.* Birmingham programme, 1919/20. This Second Division game was drawn 1-1 in front of a 14,000 crowd on 3 January 1920.

Bristol City *v.* Cardiff City, 1919/20. 'A Troubled Dream' was how P.E. Barnes perceived the worries in respect of Bristol City's FA Cup meeting with Cardiff, which was won 2-1 in front of an Ashton Gate crowd of 32,432. This appeared in the *Bristol Sports News* of 21 February 1920.

Bristol City *v.* Bradford City, 1919/20. City beat First Division Bradford City 2-0 in this FA Cup quarter-final in front of 26,443 fans at Ashton Gate on 6 March 1920. This was taken from the *Illustrated London News* of 13 March 1920.

Bristol City *v.* Huddersfield Town, 1919/20. This is how the *Bristol Sports Times* of 20 March 1920 saw City's forthcoming meeting with Huddersfield in the FA Cup semi-final at Stamford Bridge. The *Bristol Sports Times* was first published in 1909 and produced on green paper for the first time on 24 March 1917.

POPULAR AT CHELSEA. THE PENSIONER (To Bristol City): " Very pleased to see you here again, sir, and by way of a secret, I shan't be half glad if you're up here again next month for the final."

Bristol City *v.* Huddersfield Town, FA Cup semi-final programme, 1919/20.

Bristol City *v.* Huddersfield Town, 1919/20. 'All Very Well – But It Hurts!' was how the *Bristol Sports Times* of 3 April 1920 portrayed City's slightly unfortunate 1-2 defeat by Huddersfield in front of a 35,863 crowd at Stamford Bridge a week previously.

West Ham United *v*. Bristol City, 1920/21. In front of 25,000 spectators City lost this League encounter 0-1 at Upton Park on 5 March. It wasn't until 11 February 1978 that City were to win at this venue when they beat the Hammers 2-1 in a First Division fixture

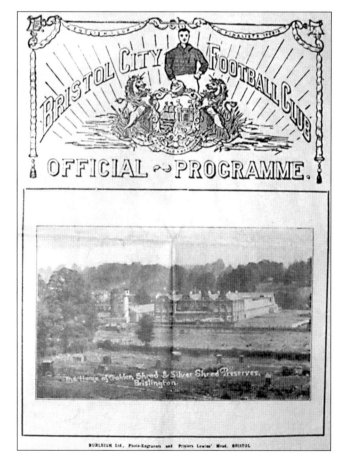

Bristol City *v*. Notts County programme, 1921/22. City drew this Second Division game 2-2 in front of a 17,000 crowd on 3 September 1921.

Souvenir card for Billy Wedlock's testimonial, 1920/21. A Bristol XI beat an International side 3-2 in front of an 8,000 Ashton Gate crowd on 4 May 1921.

'Asking For It!' from the *Bristol Sports News* of 24 December 1921. This paper, first published on 5 April 1919 and printed on pink paper since 21 August 1920, was not called the *Sports News Pink 'Un* until 25 March 1922.

Bristol City *v.* Southampton, 1923/24. Matthews of City challenges for the ball with Campell of Southampton during the Second Division game at Ashton Gate on 13 October 1923. The match was drawn 1-1 in front of 14,000 spectators. This picture appeared in the *Western Daily Press* of 15 October 1923.

'Every Picture Tells Its Story' is the title of this F.G. Lewin cartoon from the *Sports Times* of 17 April 1926 as Bristol City fall out of the promotion race.

"EVERY PICTURE TELLS ITS STORY."

PROMOTION

(Bristol City, by losing to Newport County, played the part of football "Humpty-Dumpty," and ceased to be serious candidates for Promotion.
—Drawn by Mr. F. G. LEWIN, R.W.A.

Bristol City, Third Division (South) champions, 1926/27. This official club photograph shows, from left to right, back row: W.H. Roberts (director), A.G. Wise (director), F.J. Humphries (director), F. Drewett (director), A.R.P. Bray (director), J.A. Hooper (director), C.H. Hancock (assistant secretary), A. Annan (scout). Middle row: J. Nicholson (trainer), J. Matthews (director), J. Geddes, J. Martin, T. Penn, W. Coggins, A. Jones, E. Glenn, F. Davies, A. Gray, A. Smailes, F.J. Widgery (director), L. Southway (assistant trainer). Front row: G. Jenkins (chairman), C. Gilhespy, J. Foster, G. Howson, A. Keating, H. Neesam, J. Paul, W. Wadsworth (captain), T. Walsh, A. Rankin, A. Torrance, R.G. Drummond, P.O. Daniell (vice-chairman), A.G. Raisbeck (secretary/manager). On the floor: B. Williams, R. Hughes.

'The Wisdom Of The Babe' – F.G. Lewin previews the following week's match at Luton in the *Bristol Sports Times* of 27 November 1926. The game, played on the 4 December, was a goalless draw.

Cartoons of City's 1926/27 promotion side. Note that there is an error as the positions of Tot Walsh and Jack Walsh should be reversed.

Bristol City Cricketers, 1927. City visited Midsomer Norton to play cricket on 10 August 1927. From left to right, back row: F. Drewett (director), P.O. Daniell (vice-chairman), E. Glenn, J. Pugsley, W. Coggins, C. Bourton, Alex Raisbeck (manager), G. Jenkins (chairman). Front row: J. Foster, D. Murray, J. Martin, Bert Neesam, Tot Walsh, C. Gilhespy, W.H. Roberts (director). This appeared in the *Bristol Observer* of 13 August 1927.

Chelsea captain Andy Wilson (left) and City's Johnny Paul shake hands under the watchful eye of referee T.G. Bryan prior to the goalless draw played out at Ashton Gate in front of 24,748 spectators on 22 September 1928. This photograph appeared in the *Bristol Evening News* of 24 September 1928.

A cartoonist's impression of City's 1-0 win over Preston in front of a 15,747 Ashton Gate crowd on 8 December 1928. This appeared in the *Bristol Evening News* of 11 December 1928.

The front page of *The Pink'Un* of 9 February 1929. Both the Bristol soccer clubs had won, but Bristol RFC were defeated.

IN THE SAME BOAT

'In The Same Boat' – with City and Rovers announcing losses of £5,109 and £2,703 respectively this F.G. Lewin cartoon from the *Bristol Sports Times* of 22 June 1929 warns of the stormy times that lie ahead.

A fire on the evening of 31 August 1929 destroyed much of the 'Park End' of City's No. 2 Stand. This picture was in the *Western Daily Press* of 2 September 1929.

Six
Financial Woes

Bristol City v. Romford, 1932/33. 'Keeper Pickett thwarts a rare Romford attack in front of an 8,930 crowd at Ashton Gate. City won this FA Cup first round game 4-0 on 26 November 1932.

Action from Bristol City trial game, 1930/31. In front of a 4,000 crowd Johnson (right) scores the Reds' first goal against the Whites in a 4-0 success on 18 August 1930. This picture came from the *Western Daily Press* of 19 August 1930.

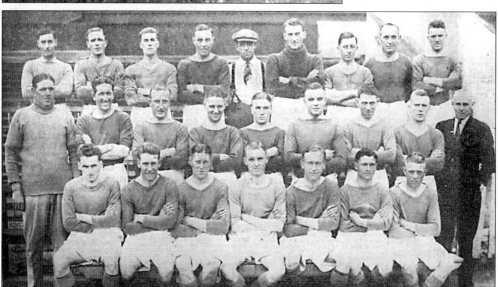

Bristol City, 1932/33. This picture appeared in the *Western Daily Press* of 29 July 1932. New manager Bob Hewison is on the extreme right of the middle row, whilst popular trainer Ernie 'Twinkle' Mellors is on the extreme left of the same row.

The start of the *Bristol Sports Post*: this advert appeared in the first edition of 23 April 1932, when Bristol City drew 0-0 at Southampton.

We take the Field

This early Bob Bennett cartoon from the *Bristol Sports Post* of 3 September 1932 depicts City's 2-0 victory over Torquay on 31 August 1932 in front of an Ashton Gate crowd of 8,762.

Bristol Sports Post, issue number 39, published on 24 December 1932.

The financially crippled City got a good response from the public as their Boxing Tourney drew a big crowd at Ashton Gate on 22 September 1933. This picture appeared in the *Bristol Evening Post* of 23 September 1933.

THE GOALKEEPER LENDS A HAND.
CAVE, the Northampton goalkeeper, fisting clear during a Bristol City raid in Saturday's game at Ashton Gate. Molloy is the City player nearest the custodian Northampton won 3—2.

Bristol City v. Northampton Town, 1933/34. Cave, the Northampton goalkeeper, fists clear during City's 2-3 defeat in this Third Division (South) game watched by 8,598 spectators on 7 October 1933.

Bristol City v. Tranmere Rovers, 1933/34. Colonel Llewellyn Williams, senior vice-president of the Welsh FA, presents the Welsh Senior Cup to the City captain, Les Birks, after Tranmere Rovers were beaten 3-0 in a replay at Sealand Road, Chester, in front of a 5,000 crowd, paying receipts of £252, on 3 May 1934.

This is Bob Bennett's cartoon of City's 5-1 win over Southend United in the last game of the season on 5 May 1934 in front of 4,323 spectators at Ashton Gate.

Bristol City AFC, with the Gloucestershire Cup and the Welsh Cup, 1934/35. This official club photograph shows, from left to right, back row: Hick, Pearce. Third row: Phipps, Roberts, Dolman, Clipson, Wilson, Webber, Cottrell. Second row: Ernie Mellors (trainer), Harston, Riley, Bridge, Hughes, Affleck, Morgan, Jenkins, Davies, Lemmo Southway (assistant trainer). Front row: Bob Hewison (manager), Cainey, Banfield, Green, Brinton, Loftus, Wallis, Foy, Fish, Moseley, C.H. Hancock (secretary). On the ground: Hodge.

Bury *v.* Bristol City, 1934/35. City pose for the cameraman before their 2-2 FA Cup draw in front of a 14,069 crowd at Bury on 16 January 1935. Left to right, back row: George Wallis, Bill Roberts, Cliff Morgan, Bill Dolman, Ernie 'Twinkle' Mellors (trainer), Cyril Bridge, Jim Pearce, Bob Hewison (manager). Front row: Jack Hodge, Jack Landells, Teddy Harston, Jimmy Loftus, Percy Cainey, Ernie Brinton.

City players taking part in FA Cup training at Ashton Gate during 1934/35.

Bristol City *v.* Portsmouth, 1934/35. City's famous FA Cup replay win over First Division Portsmouth on 30 January 1935 drew a huge crowd to Ashton Gate as these scenes from the *Bristol Evening Post* show. With many spectators breaking in, the attendance was estimated to be in excess of 50,000.

Bristol City's first but not their last appearance in the Cup Final: who's kidding who? The film of City's 1909 FA Cup final appearance was showing at the Town Hall Cinema, Bedminster, during the week commencing 4 February 1935. The film had been found in a London junk shop and purchased for 9d. Unfortunately, it appears to have been lost during the Second World War.

Bristol City players help prepare the pitch for an FA Cup meeting with Crystal Palace, which was lost 0-1 in front of a 13,997 crowd on 30 November 1935. This picture is from the *Western Daily Press* of 27 November 1935.

69

Bristol City's FA Cup heroes of 1934/35. These cartoons by Mel depict the City players who reached the fifth round before losing to Preston North End in a replay.

Bristol City *v.* Newport County, 1936/37. City beat Newport 3-1 in front of 14,467 spectators on 14 November, as shown by this Bob Bennett cartoon which appeared in the *Bristol Evening Post* two days after the match.

Bristol City *v*. Luton Town programme, 1936/37. Luton won this Third Division (South) encounter 3-2 in front of 17,193 spectators on 13 February 1937.

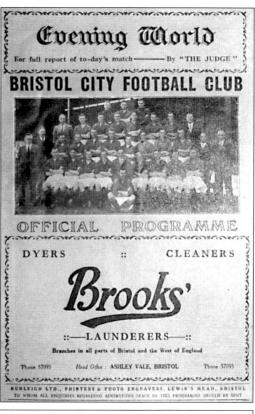

Despite winning their final game by beating Notts County in front of 13,781 Ashton Gate fans on 7 May 1938, City missed out on promotion to Millwall. This Bob Bennett cartoon was in the *Bristol Evening Post* of 9 May 1938.

Bristol City's secret trial match, 1938/39. Obviously this was not that great a secret as the *Bristol Evening Post* cameraman photographed this picture of the action on 9 August 1938.

Bristol City *v.* Notts County, 1938/39. A County defender fails to clear a low centre in City's 2-1 win at Ashton Gate in front of 17,038 fans on 7 September. This photograph appeared in the *Bristol Evening Post* of 8 September 1938.

Bristol City pre-season trial match, 1939/40. The Blues beat the Reds 4-3 in front of 3,440 spectators on 12 August 1939. Note the No. 1 Stand, which was destroyed in early 1941 by enemy action, and the tobacco bond warehouses, which were demolished in February 1995. (This photograph was taken by Geoffrey Rose.)

Bristol City v. Norwich City, 1939/40. Clarrie Bourton (right) loses the ball in an encounter with a Norwich defender as City are defeated in this Third Division (South) game 1-2 in front of an 11,544 crowd on 30 August 1939. This picture appeared in the Bristol Evening Post the following day.

Bristol City Official Programme

PRICE ONE PENNY.   KICK OFF 3.15.

NEXT HOME MATCH

WALSALL

Saturday, September 14th.

The City will field a good side
for this Match.

WALSALL HAS SOME STAR
PLAYERS IN THEIR ELEVEN.

Bristol City v. Swansea Town programme, 1940/41. For this wartime match, which City drew 1-1 in front of a 2,312 crowd, the programme confusingly advertises the next home game on the cover.

Bristol City v. Aston Villa, 1942/43. City's largest wartime crowd of 24,649 turned up for this War League Cup game on 3 April 1943. It finished as a 0-0 draw. This picture came from the Bristol Evening Post *of 5 April 1943.*

Seven
Post-War Boom

Denmark tour, 1946. This is the City side that beat the Jutland State XI 2-1 at Aarhus in front of a 3,000 crowd on 5 June 1946, thanks to goals by Bentley and Hargreaves. Left to right, back row: Ernie Jones, Ken Cousins, Ivor Guy, Don Clark, Roy Bentley, Denis Roberts, 'Lemmo' Southway (trainer). Front row: Cyril Williams, Cliff Morgan, Bill Thomas, Jack Bailey, Jack Hargreaves.

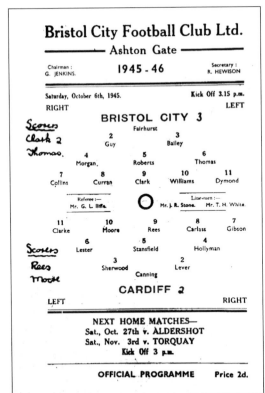

Bristol City Football Club Ltd.
—— Ashton Gate ——

Chairman : G. JENKINS.	**1945 - 46**	Secretary : R. HEWISON

Saturday, October 6th, 1945.   Kick Off 3.15 p.m.

RIGHT   LEFT

BRISTOL CITY 3

Scorers
Clark 2
Thomas.

Fairhurst

2 Guy		3 Bailey

4 Morgan.	5 Roberts	6 Thomas

7 Collins	8 Curran	9 Clark	10 Williams	11 Dymond

Referee :— Mr. G. L. Iliffe.   O   Linesmen :— Mr. J. R. Stone.   Mr. T. H. White.

11 Clarke	10 Moore	9 Rees	8 Carlass	7 Gibson

6 Lester	5 Stansfield	4 Hollyman

Scorers
Rees
Moore

3 Sherwood		2 Lever

Canning

CARDIFF 2

LEFT   RIGHT

NEXT HOME MATCHES—
Sat., Oct. 27th v. ALDERSHOT
Sat., Nov. 3rd v. TORQUAY
Kick Off 3 p.m.

OFFICIAL PROGRAMME   Price 2d.

Bristol City *v.* Cardiff City programme, 1945/46. Bristol City won this Division Three South (South Region) encounter 3-2 in front of 18,727 spectators on 6 October 1945.

Bristol City *v.* Cardiff City, 1945/46. Bristol City's Cyril Williams gets the better of Cardiff's full-back Lester to send in a header, which was well caught by 'keeper Canning. This picture comes from the *Bristol Evening Post* of 8 October 1945.

This is Bob Bennett's cartoon of City's 2-1 success against Swindon Town in a Division Three South (South Region) Cup Qualifying Competition game, which was watched by an 8,791 Ashton Gate crowd on 19 January 1946. This first appeared in the *Bristol Evening Post* of 21 January 1946.

Bristol Rovers *v.* Bristol City, 1946/47. A panoramic view of the action from the League meeting at Eastville on 28 September 1946, which City won 3-0 in front of a 25,859 crowd.

Bristol City *v.* Aldershot programme, 1946/47. City notched up their record League win with a 9-0 success in this game, played on 28 December 1946 in front of a 17,690 crowd.

Bristol City cartoons, 1946/47. These were drawn by Arthur Potts (Spot).

This 1947 centenary book was published by Bedminster Cricket Club, who played at Ashton Gate from 1898 to 1912.

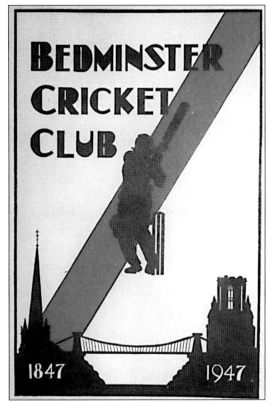

Bristol City, 1947/48. From left to right, back row: Bill Thomas, Ivor Guy, Frank Clack, Denis Roberts, Sid Kearney, Jack Bailey. Front row: Dai Hopkins, Len Townsend, Don Clark, Cyril Williams, Harry Osman.

Bristol City *v.* Swansea Town, 1947/48. Don Clark heads City's opening goal in a 3-2 Third Division (South) home win over Swansea Town on 6 September 1947 in front of a 28,068 crowd.

Bristol City *v.* Notts County, 1947/48. Despite the great Tommy Lawton towering above the City defenders to win the ball at Ashton Gate, it was City who came out on top in this Third Division game, thanks to a first-half goal from Len Townsend in front of a 35,287 crowd, who paid receipts of £2,227 16s 9d, on 3 January 1948.

Bristol City *v.* Bristol Rovers programme, 1949/50. A 16,560 crowd saw Sid Williams notch the two goals that brought victory over the old enemy in the Gloucestershire Senior Professional Cup final on 13 May 1950.

Bristol City pre-season trial match, 1950. Building work at Ashton Gate forms the backdrop to City's trial match on 12 August 1950 when the Reds beat the Whites 5-2 in front of a 9,900 crowd who paid gate receipts of £537 4s 9d.

Bristol City *v.* Gloucester City, 1950/51. City won this FA Cup clash 4-0 at Ashton Gate on 25 November 1950 in front of 17,058 spectators, who paid receipts of £1,580 11s 9d.

Bristol City *v.* Wrexham, 1950/51. This action is from City's 2-1 victory over Wrexham in the second round of the FA Cup on 9 December 1950, watched by an Ashton Gate crowd of 18,514, who paid receipts of £1,670 3s 3d.

Eight
The Atyeo Years

Bristol City *v.* Wolverhampton Wanderers, 1952/53. City's first home floodlit game, against Wolverhampton Wanderers on 27 January 1953, in front of a 23,866 crowd who paid receipts of £2,969. City lost 1-4.

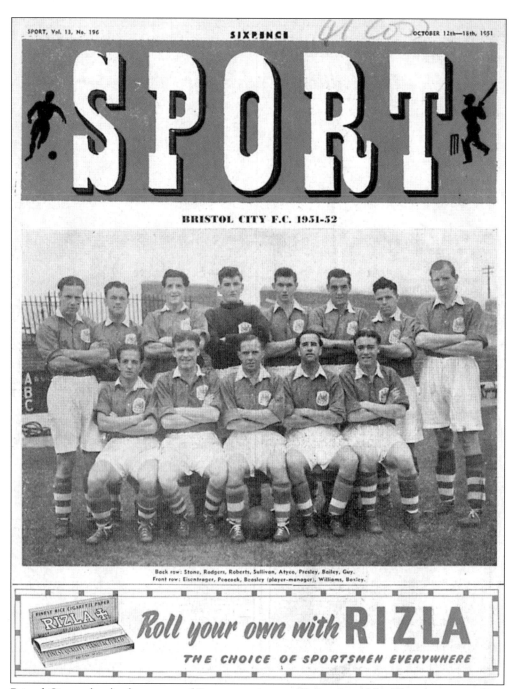

SPORT, Vol. 13, No. 196   SIXPENCE   OCTOBER 12th—18th, 1951

SPORT

BRISTOL CITY F.C. 1951-52

Back row: Stone, Rodgers, Roberts, Sullivan, Atyeo, Presley, Bailey, Guy.
Front row: Eisentrager, Peacock, Beasley (player-manager), Williams, Boxley.

Bristol City make the front page of *Sport* magazine on 12 October 1951. The players are, from left to right, back row: Stone, Rodgers, Roberts, Sullivan, Atyeo, Presley, Bailey, Guy. Front row: Eisentrager, Peacock, Beasley (player-manager), Williams, Boxley.

Bristol City *v.* Crystal Palace, 1952/53. Cyril Williams heads in one of his three goals in City's 5-0 Third Division (South) win over Crystal Palace in front of a 17,163 crowd at Ashton Gate crowd on 13 September 1952.

Bristol City *v.* Rotherham United, 1953/54. John Atyeo, playing in the Rovers' blue and white quartered shirts, in action against Rotherham United in the FA Cup on 9 January 1954 when a 29,216 Ashton Gate crowd saw City lose 1-3.

Another view of John Atyeo in unfamiliar blue and white quarters against Rotherham on 9 January 1954. Atyeo again turned out in Rovers' colours four years later when City played Accrington Stanley in the FA Cup.

Bristol City v. Millwall, 1953/54. John Atyeo scores in City's 2-0 home success in front of 14,618 spectators against Millwall on 19 April 1954.

A fine action photograph of
Atyeo against unknown
opponents in the mid-1950s.

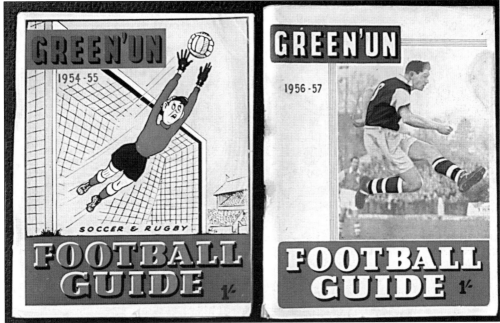

Green'Un football guides, 1954/55 and 1956/57. Bristol sports followers were spoilt for choice
in the early years after the war with annual publications for soccer, speedway and cricket.

Watford *v.* Bristol City, 1954/55. John Atyeo fires City's final goal in a 2-0 success over Watford in front of a 15,850 Vicarage Road crowd on 2 April 1955.

City are presented with the Third Division (South) Championship Shield by Arthur Oakley in front of 27,726 crowd, after their 0-0 home draw with Newport County on 23 April 1955. The City players are, from left to right: Jack Boxley, John Atyeo, Jimmy Rogers, Harry Dolman (chairman), Bob Anderson, Ernie Peacock, Jack White.

Crystal Palace *v.* Bristol City, 1954/55. This photograph was taken prior to City's 2-1 win in front of a 14,425 crowd at Selhurst Park on 30 April 1955. From left to right, back row: Cyril Williams, Ivor Guy, Bob Anderson, John Atyeo, Arthur Milton, Mike Thresher. Front row: Ernie Peacock, Jimmy Rogers, Jackie White, Tommy Burden, Jack Boxley.

Bristol Rovers *v.* Bristol City, 1954/55. Bob Anderson makes a fine save against his former Bristol Rovers team-mates, but he is unable to prevent City losing at Eastville 1-2 in front of a record Gloucestershire Senior Professional Cup crowd of 20,097 on 2 May 1955.

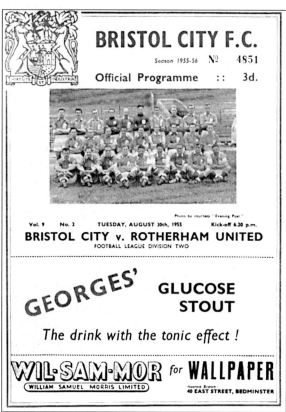

Bristol City *v*. Rotherham United
programme, 1955/56. City won this
Division Two game against
Rotherham United 5-2 on
30 August 1955 in front of a 27,142
crowd.

Bristol City *v.* West Ham United, 1955/56. John Atyeo makes his presence felt as City beat the
Hammers 3-1 in front of a 25,993 Ashton Gate crowd on 6 September 1955.

Bristol City *v*. Bury, 1955/56. John Atyeo scores from the spot in front of a 22,949 crowd during City's 3-0 home Second Division success over Bury on 17 September 1955. The other City players in view are Alec Eisentrager (left) and Tommy Burden (middle).

Bristol City *v*. Hull City, 1955/56. John Atyeo in action during City's 5-2 home win over Hull City, watched by 22,776 fans on 5 November 1955.

Jimmy Rogers scores in the 5-2 victory over Hull on 5 November 1955.

Bristol City *v.* Sheffield Wednesday, 1955/56. Jimmy Rogers, hidden by the left-back, is about to score City's winning goal against Sheffield Wednesday at Ashton Gate on 19 November 1955. A crowd of 32,731 were present to see City win 3-2 to go top of the Second Division table.

Bristol City *v.* Lincoln City, 1955/56. In front of a 26,329 crowd, Jimmy Rogers scores in City's 5-1 Division Two win over Lincoln on 3 December 1955.

Bristol Rovers *v.* Bristol City, 1955/56. John Atyeo runs in to shoulder charge Bristol Rovers 'keeper Ron Nicholls over the line for City's first goal in a 3-0 Division Two success in front of a 35,198 Eastville crowd on 3 March 1956.

Bristol City *v.* Bristol Rovers
programme, 1956/57. City won this
high-scoring Division Two derby 5-3 in
front of 37,207 spectators on
22 September 1956.

Bristol Rovers *v.* Bristol City, 1956/57. City's Ernie Peacock moves in to protect 'keeper Bob
Anderson from the attention of the marauding Alfie Biggs in a Second Division 0-0 draw in
front of a 32,055 crowd at Eastville on 2 February 1957.

City star Wally Hinshelwood played for the club from 1956 to 1960. This photograph shows Bristol City's scintillating winger, who on his day could rival the great Stanley Matthews, in action during a 3-0 FA Cup success over giant-killers Rhyl.

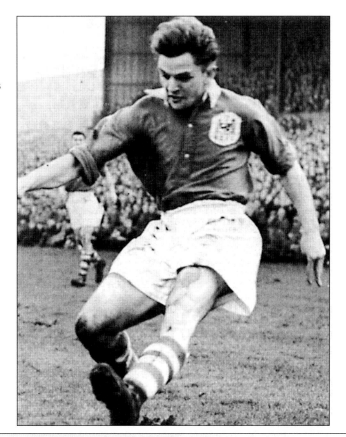

Bristol City v. Rhyl, 1956/57. John Atyeo scores one of his two goals in City's 3-0 defeat of Rhyl in the fourth round of the FA Cup in front of a 29,438 Ashton Gate crowd on 26 January 1957.

Aston Villa *v*. Bristol City, 1956/57. John Atyeo scores the goal he rated as the best he ever netted as injury-hit City succumbed to a 1-2 FA Cup defeat in front of a 63,099 Villa Park crowd on 16 February 1957. This picture graced the front cover of City's programme throughout the 1957/58 and 1958/59 seasons.

Aston Villa *v*. Bristol City programme, 1956/57. After beating City in this fifth round game Villa went on to win the FA Cup.

Atyeo for England! England captain Billy Wright introduces Earl Mountbatten to Stanley Matthews before an international match, watched by City's John Atyeo and Fulham's Johnny Haynes.

England v. Republic of Ireland, 1957. City's John Atyeo heads in England's third goal in a 5-1 victory over the Republic of Ireland at Wembley in this World Cup qualifying match on 8 May.

Republic of Ireland *v.* England, 1957. John Atyeo in action during his final international on 19 May 1957, when his headed goal in the dying seconds against the Republic of Ireland in Dublin earned a 1-1 draw to take England through to the World Cup finals.

Bristol City *v.* Derby County programme, 1957/58. A 17,090 crowd, who were attracted to Ashton Gate on this the last occasion that City played on Christmas Day, witnessed a 2-1 home success.

Barnsley *v.* Bristol City programme, 1958/59. City won this Second Division game 7-4 in front of 14,283 spectators at Oakwell on 27 August 1958.

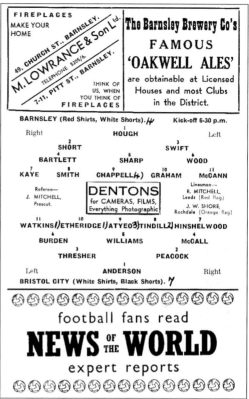

Bristol City *v.* Scunthorpe United, 1958/59. A Bob Bennett cartoon depicting third-placed City's shock 0-1 home defeat by bottom of the table Scunthorpe United in front of a 20,306 Ashton Gate crowd on 22 November 1958. This appeared in the *Evening Post* on 24 November 1958.

How the *Pink 'Un* covered Stanley Matthews' visit to play for Blackpool at Ashton Gate on 24 January 1959. The largest post-war attendance at this venue of 42,594 witnessed a thrilling 1-1 draw in the fourth round of the FA Cup.

Bristol City, 1958/59. Left to right, back row: Alan Williams, Gordon Hopkinson, John Atyeo, Tony Cook, Peter McCall, Mike Thresher. Front row: Derek Virgin, Bert Tindill, Tommy Burden, Bobby Etheridge, Johnny Watkins.

Tony Cook was an outstanding 'keeper renowned for saving penalties. He played for City from 1949 until 1964. In this picture, taken during the famous cup-tie with Blackpool on 24 January 1959, he watches the ball sail over the bar.

Bert Tindill, City's capture from Doncaster Rovers in February 1958, provided the goals that saved City from relegation. He was transferred to Barnsley in the close season of 1959.

Mike Thresher, a fierce tackling full-back, effectively shackled the great Stanley Matthews at Ashton Gate in January 1959.

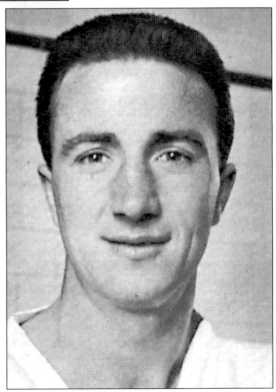

Tommy Casey was already a well-established Irish international wing-half and an FA Cup winner with Newcastle United in 1955 when he joined City from Portsmouth in 1959.

Bristol City *v.* Middlesbrough, 1959/60. Centre half Alan Williams played centre forward in this Second Division game on 26 September 1959 and scored in City's 2-0 success in front of a 21,640 crowd.

BRISTOL CITY F.C.

SEASON 1959-60

4 D.

Sat. 26th Sept. MIDDLESBROUGH Div. 2 K.O. 3.0 p.m.

• OFFICIAL PROGRAMME •

Bristol City *v.* Derby County, 1959/60. John Atyeo heads wide in this 0-1 defeat in front of 14,055 Ashton Gate fans on 20 February 1960.

Bristol Rovers v. Bristol City, 1959/60. Malcolm Graham's shot is blocked against Bristol Rovers in City's 1-2 Second Division defeat in front of 27,039 fans at Eastville on 27 February 1960.

BRISTOL CITY FOOTBALL CLUB LIMITED

F.A. Youth Cup Semi-Final First Leg

Bristol City Youths

v.

Chelsea Youths

Tuesday, April 5th   K.O. 7.30 p.m.

BRISTOL CITY YOUTHS

RIGHT   Colours : Red and White   LEFT

H. BOOTH

HUXFORD—2   M. THOMAS—3

DAVIS, J.—4   QUINLAN—5   PREWETT—6

R. PETERS—7   CLARK—8   BUSH—9   A. WILLIAMS—10   DERRICK—11

Referee :   Linesmen :
J. FINNEY   K. C. Hanham (Wilts.)
(Hereford)   W. J. Paradise (Som.)

HARKNESS—9
TAMBLING—11 G. BOLLAND—10   C. SHAW—8 A. MURRAY—7
M. ROBINSON—6   T. MORE—5   T. VENABLES—4
A. HARRIS—3   D. BUTLER—2
BONETTI

LEFT   Colours : Blue and White   RIGHT

CHELSEA YOUTHS

Souvenir Programme

Bristol City Youth v. Chelsea Youth programme, 1959/60. Bristol City had their record youth game attendance of 18,181 for this semi-final, which they lost 0-3 on 5 April 1960.

Bristol City, 1959/60. The 'split camp' side photographed just prior to kick-off in the home 2-3 defeat by Rotherham United, watched by a 20,407 crowd on 29 August 1959. From left to right, back row: Gordon Hopkinson, Jimmy Rogers, Bobby Etheridge, Tony Cook, Tommy Cavanagh, Tommy Casey. Front row: Wally Hinshelwood, John Atyeo, Tommy Burden, Mike Thresher, John McCann.

Aston Villa v. Bristol City, 1959/60. John Atyeo shoots for goal in City's unlucky 1-2 defeat against Division Two leaders Aston Villa in front of a 33,556 crowd at Villa Park on 9 April 1960. This picture comes from the *Birmingham Sports Argus* of the same day.

Bristol City *v.* Stoke City, 1959/60. Jantzen Derrick centres in this end-of-season game which City lost 1-2 in front of 9,013 spectators on 30 April 1960. (This photograph was taken by David Woods.)

City brought the curtain down on a disappointing season by beating Bristol Rovers 3-2 in front of a 7,195 Ashton Gate crowd on 2 May 1960 to win the Gloucestershire Senior Professional Cup. This trophy, which had been competed for since the 1887/88 season, was replaced with a new cup in 1967/68.

Jimmy Rogers, an energetic, goalscoring forward, had two lengthy spells with Bristol City (1950 to 1956 and 1958 to 1962) interrupted by a couple of seasons at Coventry.

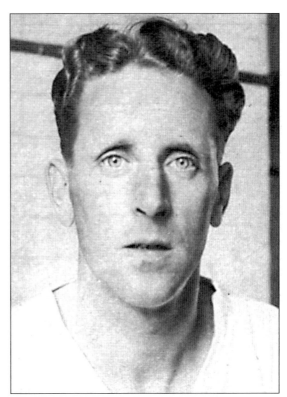

Jantzen Derrick, a wing wizard, became Bristol City's youngest player when he made his debut in a 1-3 defeat at Lincoln City on 28 November 1959 at the age of 16 years 324 days. He played for City until 1971.

ONE SHILLING   SOCCER STAR, May 14, 1960   VOL. 8   NO. 34

★ *Two teams on the cover every week*

SOCCER STAR

BRISTOL CITY: Left to right (back row): A. Williams, R. Collinson, R. Etheridge, A. Cook, T. Casey, M. Thresher. (Front): J. Rogers, T. Burden, J. Atyeo, M. Graham, J. McCann. (W.1).

coming in next week's edition :

● The United States International Soccer League starts in New York on May 25 and SOCCER STAR is running a front cover series of the competitors. Number one, next week, is SAMPDORIA. On the back cover is a late season picture of ROTHERHAM (back cover foreign teams start on June 4). Eric Batty previews in word and pictures the coming HUNGARY v ENGLAND international in Budapest. A number of new summer features will begin, among them GREAT TEAMS by S. Hall who spotlights with rare photos romantic stories of England's top teams.

A Bristol City picture from the back page of the *Soccer Star* of 14 May 1960 showing the side that lost at Villa Park on 9 April 1960. Left to right, back row: Alan Williams, Roger Collinson, Bobby Etheridge, Tony Cook, Tommy Casey, Mike Thresher. Front row: Jimmy Rogers, Tommy Burden, John Atyeo, Malcolm Graham, John McCann.

Nine
The Ford Era

Bristol City, 1960/61. This photograph was taken at Keynsham Town FC, where City carried out their pre-season training. From left to right, back row: Roger Collinson, Tommy Casey, Bobby Etheridge, Tony Cook, Mike Thresher, John McCann, Pete McCall. Front row: Alan Williams, Jimmy Rogers, Alex Tait, John Atyeo, John 'Buck' Ryan, Jantzen Derrick.

Bristol City *v.* Bournemouth & Boscombe Athletic, 1960/61. In front of a 14,455 crowd, paying receipts of £1,945 16s 0d, Jantzen Derrick's late goal brought City a fortunate 1-0 success in their first home match in the Third Division.

Bristol City *v.* Hull City, 1960/61. John Atyeo's goal is disallowed in this 1-2 home defeat in front of 14,899 spectators on 24 September 1960.

Further action from the game against Hull as John Atyeo fails to meet this cross.

HAVING HEARD THAT THE CITY'S VISITORS CAME FROM THE BIRTHPLACE OF JOE DAVIS —WE EXPECTED SOME EXTRAORDINARY SCORING

FROM CHESTERFIELD ON SATURDAY —WE

ANTICIPATED THAT THEY WOULD SNOOKER

THE CITY IN THE FIRST MINUTE— THEN THEY WOULD GET THE BREAKS-

—AND SINK THE REDS IN NO TIME —BUT

ALAS— CHESTERFIELD EITHER MISCUED IN FRONT OF GOAL

OR WERE BAULKED BY THE CITY DEFENCE

THEY COULD HAVE MADE GOOD USE OF A LONG REST AFTER THE INTERVAL— AND WE ARE AFRAID THAT THE CITY

DID ALL THE SUCCESSFUL POTTING IN THIS MATCH —SPEED.

Speed's cartoon from the *Evening World* of City's 3-0 Third Division home win over Chesterfield in front of 7,796 spectators on 22 October 1960.

Coverage from the *Pink 'Un* of City's record 11-0 FA Cup victory over Chichester City on 5 November 1960. The game was watched by a crowd of 12,588.

Bristol City in 1960/61, as featured on the back page of the *Soccer Star* of 14 January 1961. From left to right, back row: Hopkinson, Derrick, McCall. Middle row: Casey, Williams, Etheridge, Cook, Anderson, Burden, Collinson. Front: Ryan, Rogers, Atyeo, Tait, McCann.

Bristol City *v.* Swindon Town, 1961/62. John Atyeo's shot evades the visitor's 'keeper in City's thrilling 5-3 Division Three success on 21 October 1961.

Bristol City *v.* Swindon Town, 1961/62. A few seconds later John Atyeo's shot crossed the line in City's 5-3 win over Swindon Town in front of 13,158 spectators at Ashton Gate on 21 October 1961.

Bristol City *v.* Peterborough United, 1961/62. John Atyeo's headed goal is not enough as, in front of a 17,123 crowd, City go down to a 1-2 Third Division defeat at the hands of the visitors on 13 January.

Bristol City *v.* Lincoln City, 1961/62. Alex Tait celebrates in front a 12,190 crowd as City score in their 2-0 Third Division success on 3 February 1962.

Bristol City *v.* Bradford Park Avenue, 1961/62. City are on the attack at the Open End in front of 16,217 spectators during their spectacular 6-1 home success over Bradford Park Avenue on 10 February 1962. Atyeo (8) and Tait are the City players in view.

Another view of the Third Division clash against Bradford with Tait, Atyeo and Rogers leading City's attack on the Covered End goal.

The *Green 'Un* records City's 6-1 home win over Bradford Park Avenue.

Bristol City *v.* Watford, 1961/62. City attack during a 2-1 Third Division home win against Watford on 3 March 1962. The game was watched by 11,983 spectators.

Bristol City *v*. Halifax Town, 1961/62. A crowded goalmouth as City attack the Halifax citadel in an exciting 4-3 Ashton Gate success in front of 6,807 fans on 14 April 1962.

Bristol City *v*. Crystal Palace, 1961/62. Roger 'Lou' Peters (out of picture) scores in City's 2-2 Third Division draw with Crystal Palace in front of a 7,199 Ashton Gate crowd on 28 April 1962.

Bristol City Reserves, 1961/62. The players are, from left to right: Gordon Parr, Tony Cook, Geoff Palmer, Peter McCall, Jantzen Derrick, Steve Stacey, David Noake, Terry Bush and Adrian Williams. They are displaying the Western League Cup, which they won 9-1 on aggregate after beating Dorchester Town 5-1 in the second leg of the final at Ashton Gate on 3 May 1962. In previous rounds, Weston-super-Mare had been beaten 4-1 after a 3-3 draw, then Bristol Rovers Colts were dispatched 2-1, before Glastonbury were overcome in the semi-final 5-0.

Bristol City, 1962/63. Left to right, back row: Adrian Williams, David Pyle, Tony Ford, Tony Cook, Terry Bush, Brian Clark, David Smith, Pete Laverick, Tommy Casey. Middle row: Steve Stacey, Alec Briggs, Bobby Etheridge, Mike Thresher, Jack Connor, Gordon Low, Les Bardsley (physiotherapist). Front row: Arthur Proudler (coach), Roger 'Lou' Peters, Ray Savino, John Atyeo, Alex Tait, Bobby Williams, Jantzen Derrick, Gordon Parr, Fred Ford (manager).

Combined Bristol XI *v.* Arsenal, 1962/63. John Atyeo (in white) challenges the Arsenal 'keeper McKechnie in the St Mary Redcliffe Restoration Appeal game at Ashton Gate on 8 August 1962. A crowd of 19,962, paying receipts of £3,400, turned up to see a Combined Bristol XI (five Rovers players and six City) lose 1-2.

Bristol City *v.* Millwall, 1962/63. John Atyeo scores against Millwall in the opening Third Division game of the season on 18 August 1962. However, City could only manage a 2-2 draw in front of 14,049 fans at Ashton Gate.

Bristol City *v.* Port Vale, 1962/63. John Atyeo (9) watches the Port Vale 'keeper secure the ball despite the challenge of Derek Lythgoe in City's 2-0 Ashton Gate win in front of 9,626 fans on 1 September 1962.

Bristol City *v.* Reading, 1962/63. Jantzen Derrick scores City's second goal in a 4-2 success over Reading in the final League game of the season on 18 May 1963. A crowd of 7,043 were thrilled to see City notch up a total of 100 League goals for the season, despite finishing in fourteenth place.

Bristol City *v.* Oldham Athletic, 1963/64. John Atyeo (9) in goalmouth action for City during their 3-1 victory over Oldham Athletic on 29 February 1964 in front of a 9,900 Ashton Gate crowd.

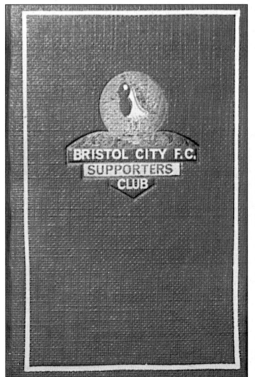

Bristol City Supporters Club membership booklets. There was considerable variation in design during the 1960s.

PRICE 6d.

THE FUTURE OF BRISTOL CITY

By Harry Dolman

New Club is A Big Hit

Extra Comforts For fans

The Robins Club in the main stand — it opened a few weeks ago — is already a firm favourite with season ticket holders.

Here no-r another club has it all the West Country. For everyone who buys a ticket for the season is not materially able for election to member ship.

The Board has long recog nised the charming nature of soccer habits. The '51 Club for instance, was formed years ahead of similar ventures and with the Robins Club we have scored another notable first.

Opening before the game, at half-time and afterwards, pre-sented obvious problems, is serving a rush of people in a short time but looking after them in comfort.

"When you drink and gossip you want something to lean on," he explained, "so I set out to provide comfortable padding on the bars, and set the tables plus a warm, light 'clubby' atmosphere.

A feature everyone is talking about, the two giant murals blowing up from scenes taken at the Cup-tie with Brighton in November.

Several thousand proudly have gone into the new build ing, it's all part of City's cam paign to make Ashton Gate the No. 1 Sporting Social centre of the West.

The Club committee Chairman, Fred Callow is founder member of the '51 Club.

Secretary, Bert Bush Members Bill Febry, Ted Crew and Len Smart with Bob Purton as bar men officers between club and the Board.

Workmen put the final touches to the huge mural which decorates the Robins Club.

Floodlights In 1878

Bristol City were one of the pioneers of floodlighting but how many people know when the first match was played under lights?

It was at Bramall Lane, Sheffield, on October 14th, 1878. Power was generated from behind each goal and lights were on 16 foot poles at each corner.

But nearly 80 years went by before the first floodlit league game was played — between Portsmouth and Newcastle at Fratton Park, February 22nd, 1956.

NEW STAND PLANNED

PLANS for Ashton Gate have been discussed by the Board. They include a new stand and floodlighting but these are long term plans; the immediate aim is a higher class football.

"We spend thousands every year on the ground", says chairman Harry Dolman. "We're very much aware that public tastes are changing.

"People following football are looking for higher standards of entertainment and comfort.

"Every penny we receive is ploughed back into the club with these objects in view".

BEFORE the season began I prophesied that 1965 would be a promotion year for Bristol City. Whatever the outcome is finally, there is one thing I want to make clear on behalf of the Board: our deter-mination and thoughts are directed in one direction only — to lead the club we love to a leading place in the English football scene.

A few weeks ago, in the death of Billy Wedlock we lost a link with the glorious past, a link with those fine years when we were one of the great sides of the First Division.

The way back, even to the spring-board of the Sec-ond Division, is hard and heavy with disappoint-ment. But we must make it.

Bristol is growing fast. The capital of the West will become even more important in the years ahead.

Football must keep pace. Here at Ashton Gate we are ideally situated. We own our ground which compares favourably with many in the country. We run, think and plan like a First Division club.

Fred Ford is bringing along a group of younger players who are the envy of sides in higher divisions.

Our new Robins Club, the backing of our 51 Club members, the happy relationships with our Supporters Club, the efforts of our agents selling tickets for the various fund-raising schemes — all these things point to a bright and vigorous future.

Not TWO Young To Cheer City

CITY'S youngest fan was registered as a member of the Supporters' Club seconds after birth.

Now 21 months old, fair-haired Robert Bidgood goes to most home matches with his parents Mr. Roy Bidgood — on the Supporters' Club committee — and wife Margaret of Jacque Street, Bedminster.

Robert is trundled down to the ground in his push-chair, sits on his father's shoulders and has learned to shout "goal" and "foul". His favour-ite player is "Big John" — John Atyeo.

Two other young Bidgoods join in the cheering — daughters Susan, aged 5, and Jennifer, 4, both of whom were made supporters by Mr. Roy, good minutes after they were born.

ROBERT

LARGEST TYRE SERVICE IN THE WEST

COUNTY TYRE SERVICE (BRISTOL) LTD.

The Robin, 1964/65. This first issue was produced for the Bristol derby on 13 February 1965 when a 23,053 crowd saw City beat the division's leaders 2-1.

Bristol City, 1964/65. Left to right, back row: Brian Thurlow, Jack Connor, Mike Gibson, Chuck Drury, Gordon Low. Middle row: Alec Briggs, Steve Stacey, Terry Bush, Bobby Etheridge, Mike Thresher, Tony Ford. Front row: Jantzen Derrick, Brian Clark, John Atyeo, Bobby Williams, Ray Savino, Peter Hooper. On the floor: Roger 'Lou' Peters, Gerry Sharpe, Gordon Parr. Inset: Ron Nicholls.

Bristol City *v.* Hull City, 1964/65. Hull's 'keeper Mike Milner safely gathers the ball despite the imposing presence of John Atyeo during City's 1-2 home defeat, watched by 14,131 fans, on 23 January 1965.

Bristol City *v.* Oldham Athletic, 1964/65. John Atyeo, out of picture, scores City's second goal in the vital win over Oldham Athletic that clinched promotion in front of a 28,248 Ashton Gate crowd on 24 April 1965.

The *Green' Un*'s coverage of City's promotion on 24 April 1965.

Bristol City *v.* Bolton Wanderers, 1965/66. John Atyeo scores in City's 2-2 Second Division draw with Bolton Wanderers in front of a 19,912 crowd at Ashton Gate on 13 November 1965.

Jovial centre half Jack Connor achieved cult status at Ashton Gate after signing from Huddersfield Town in a swap deal involving City winger John McCann. He played for City from 1960 until 1971.

Mike Gibson was probably the best goalkeeper City have ever had. Signed from Shrewsbury Town, he gave superb service from 1963 until 1972 before joining Gillingham.

One of City's four floodlight pylons being erected in December 1965. The opening of Ashton Gate's second floodlight system coincided with the visit of Wolves for a League game on 28 December 1965 – when City lost their unbeaten home record by going down 0-1 in front of a 36,184 crowd. These pylons, topped by their distinctive angled heads, remained a feature of the Ashton Gate skyline until being removed in June 1992, whereupon they saw further service at Wigan Athletic's Springfield Park home. City's original floodlight system was purchased by Burton Albion.

This action is from from City's 1-1 friendly draw with First Division Southampton on 13 August 1966, which attracted a 6,903 crowd to a strange-looking Ashton Gate following the demolition of the old Number Two Stand in the close season.

Bristol City Football Club Ltd.

ASHTON GATE FIXTURES

WEDNESDAY, NOVEMBER 16th   **Kick-off 7.30**

SPECIAL ATTRACTION - INTER-CITY CUP MATCH

HANOVER 96

Usual First Team Prices   **All Pay**

MID-WEEK MATCHES COMPLETED UNDER FLOODLIGHTS

ADMISSION PRICES. Ground (uncovered) 4/-; Ground (covered) 4/6; Enclosures 5/-; Ringside 6/-; Grand Stand 12/-. All seats bookable in advance.
Juveniles admitted at half-price in Ground and Enclosures.   O.A.P.s admitted to Ground for 2/6

Special bus services run from all parts of the City and Suburbs

Accommodation for over **20,000** under cover

Commentaries of all 1st team home matches relayed to Bristol Hospitals

Posters of this design, with red lettering on a white background displaying a list of a forthcoming Ashton Gate fixtures (first team, reserves, colts and youths), were a feature of the street scene during the 1950s and 1960s. Unfortunately, this sole survivor has been truncated to show only one attraction – the Friendship Cup (donated by the *Bristol Evening Post*), which City lost 2-3 in front of a 4,599 crowd on 16 November 1966. Bristol Rovers produced similar posters although, of course, their lettering was blue.

A skilful trio of 1966/67 signings. From left to right: Chris Crowe (Nottingham Forest), Hugh McIlmoyle (Wolverhampton Wanderers), John Quigley (Huddersfield Town).

Acknowledgements

It was the recent publication of the Bristol Rovers book in The *Archive Photographs* Series that made me think that my collection of Bristol City photographs would be of interest to the public.

However, the fact that my photographic library has been greatly enhanced over the years by other fans allowing me to copy their collections, has required this work be split into two parts.

I am indebted to local football historian and author David Woods, particularly in regard to the pre-Second World War years, as he has contributed much to my collection in addition to others such as Mervyn Baker, Mick Hunter, Mike Jay, Malcolm Norman, Gerry Pearce, Matthew Stevens, Roly Stubbins, Mike Swain and Steve Tuckfield, whose large archives have done so much to keep my interest alive.

Thanks are also offered to Ron Cranfield, Bill Davies, Jantzen Derrick, Leigh Edwards, H.J. Kelson, Monica Spencer (daughter of the Bedminster and Bristol South End winger Frank Mayger), James Thomas, Alan Williams and David Wring for photographs which they have supplied.

Appreciation is also due to the many sporting cartoonists whose work was once such a regular feature in the local newspapers, amongst whom over the years have been: Samuel Loxton, F.G. Lewin, Phil Barnes (Quip), Bob Bennett, Arthur Potts (Spot) and Jim Neal (Speed). Hopefully, this way of recording the local sporting scene, which has all but died out since Bob Bennett's retirement in the mid-1960s, will be revived by those such as Paul Thatcher whose drawings in the Bristol City programme in 1999/2000 were such a delight.

Finally, a big thank you to the founding fathers of Bristol City of whom some are included in the photograph below, which appeared in the *Bristol Sports Post* of 9 July 1932.

Bristol City directors, 1899/1900. From left to right, back row: E.C. Tyack, William Panes Kingston (chairman), Albert E. Denby, George J. Maggs, Walter G. Tozer, Harry Locke (financial secretary). Front row: Bob Campbell (secretary/manager), E.H. Webb, F.H. 'Harry' King, James Crompton (vice-chairman), F.H. Hawksby, Joseph Daveridge.